COWBOYS & LONGHORNS

For Mark

JERRY STANLEY
COWBOYS
& LONGHORNS

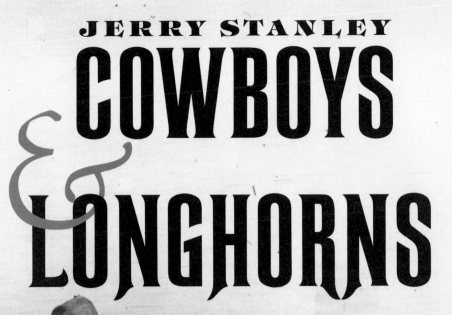

CROWN PUBLISHERS
NEW YORK

Published by Crown Publishers, an imprint of Random House Children's Books,
a division of Random House, Inc., New York.

CROWN and colophon are trademarks of Random House, Inc.

www.randomhouse.com/kids

Library of Congress Cataloging-in-Publication Data
Stanley, Jerry. 1941–
Cowboys and longhorns : a portrait of the long drive / by Jerry Stanley.
p.   cm.
Includes bibliographical references and index.
ISBN 0-375-81565-1 (trade) — ISBN 0-375-91565-6 (lib. bdg.)
1. Cowboys—West (U.S.)—History—19th century—Juvenile literature. 2. Longhorn
cattle—West (U.S.)—History—19th century—Juvenile literature. 3. Cattle drives—West
(U.S.)—History—19th century—Juvenile literature. 4. West (U.S.)—History—
1860–1890—Juvenile literature. 5. West (U.S.)—Social life and customs—
19th century—Juvenile literature. 6. Texas, West—History—19th century—
Juvenile literature. 7. Texas, West—Social life and customs—19th
century—Juvenile literature. I. Title.
F596 .S824 2003
636.2'13'0976409034—dc21
2002041229
Printed in the United States of America
August 2003
10 9 8 7 6 5 4 3 2 1
First Edition

Contents

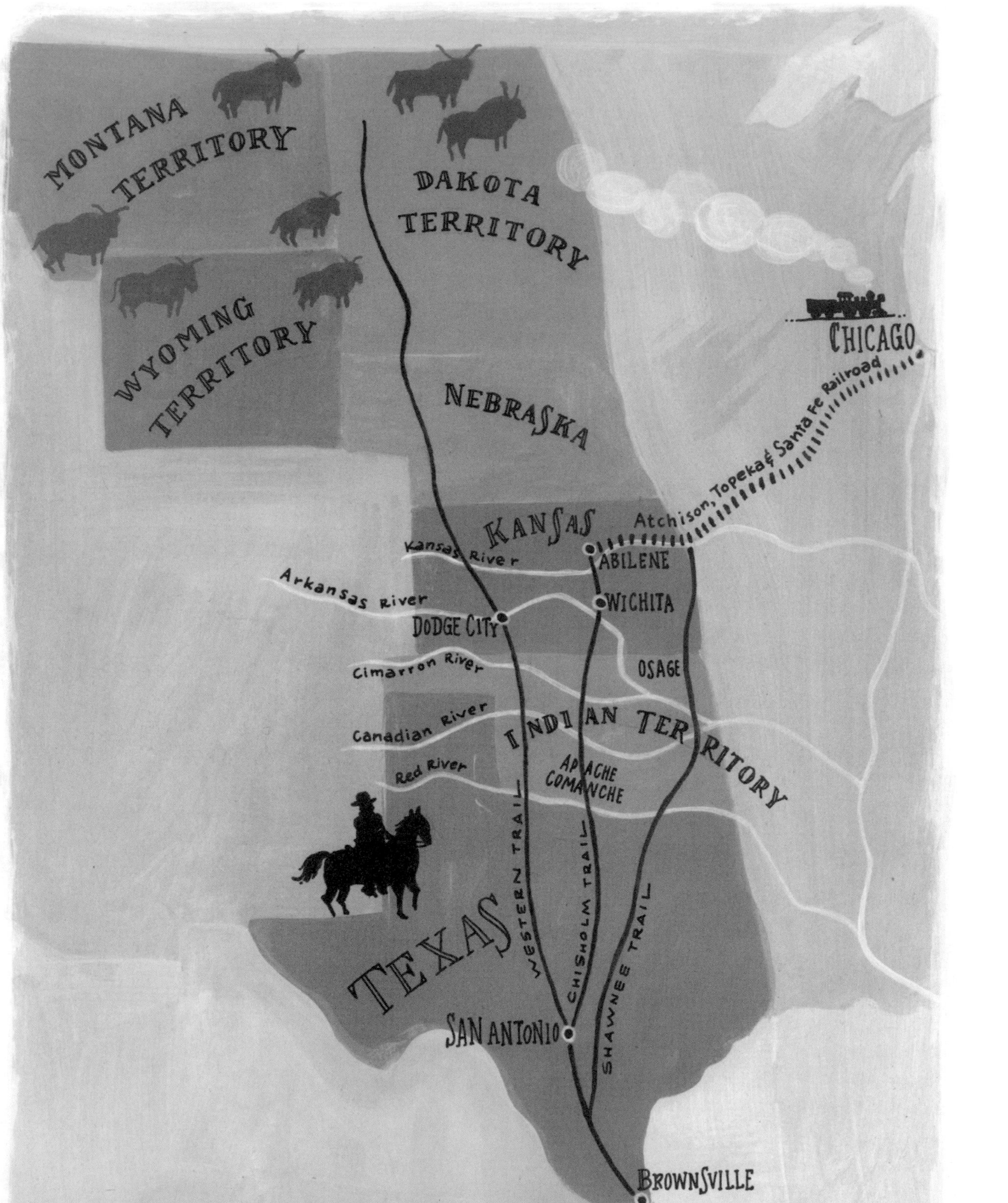
MONTANA TERRITORY
DAKOTA TERRITORY
WYOMING TERRITORY
NEBRASKA
CHICAGO
Atchison, Topeka & Santa Fe Railroad
KANSAS
Kansas River
ABILENE
Arkansas River
WICHITA
DODGE CITY
Cimarron River
OSAGE
Canadian River
INDIAN TERRITORY
Red River
APACHE
COMANCHE
WESTERN TRAIL
CHISHOLM TRAIL
SHAWNEE TRAIL
TEXAS
SAN ANTONIO
BROWNSVILLE

Of all the characters in American history, one stands out as the most popular and visible: the cowboy. While politicians and celebrities come and go, the image of the cowboy has persisted for more than a hundred years. He is still seen every day in music, dance, advertising, dress, sports, and the movies, and his history is memorialized in the Cowboy Hall of Fame. He is almost always picked to lead parades. Handsomely dressed on a well-groomed horse, he smiles and waves to the crowd.

Gregory Peck dressed as Hollywood's idea of a cowboy. From the film *Duel in the Sun.*

The cowboy image is popular because the cowboy supposedly possessed the characteristics of a true American. He was independent, but he stood for order. He was violent, but he stood for justice. Many people think that he symbolized the American spirit, that he was strong, confident, brave, and content, and that he liked being a cowboy.

But many historians believe that the image of the cowboy in the popular mind has caused great harm to America. Because the cowboy is portrayed as white, some Americans see him as an example of the superiority of the white race. Because he is depicted as violent, some Americans have used him to celebrate violence. The

A *real* cowboy.

cowboy is shown as conquering nature without a thought to the environment, and he has been used as an enduring symbol of the dominance of men over women. (In most cowboy movies of fifty years ago, a woman obeyed the cowboy's every command, and he ended up loving his horse more than her.)

It was no accident that the cowboy was used for these purposes, historians say, and some argue that modern dramas on television and film depict the same themes: good guys versus bad guys, using violence as a way of resolving conflicts, and the continuing role of women as secondary to men. In other words, what the cowboy has been made to represent is as popular as ever.

The truth is that *real* cowboys did not think of themselves as good or bad, and if they could see a modern cowboy leading a parade, they would fall off their horses laughing. For starters, a cowboy wasn't independent but worked as part of an organized unit. He was most often tired and bored, and he usually quit cowboy life after a few short months. He was concerned with controlling animals, not with being brave and content. He was concerned with staying alive, not with achieving justice. If he fought Indians, it was because he had no other choice. If he didn't talk much, it was because he couldn't be heard over the sound of three thousand cattle pounding the earth. The cowboy was a hired hand on a hired horse. His life revolved around a specific animal—an animal never encountered by fictional cowboys.

This is the true story of cowboys and longhorns, a breed of cattle that created the American cowboy. It is about a relationship that existed between humans and an animal for about twenty years, from 1866 to 1885. It was a difficult relationship and always unpredictable, and it has been ignored in portrayals of the cowboy. As a result, the purpose of the cowboy has been distorted. He has been made into some kind of hero, when that was the last thing he had in mind.

An artist's conception of a cattle drive from the 1800s.

The cowboy's job was to capture longhorns, a wild animal that was fiercely independent, and then he had to control them. He stayed with the longhorns for about eight months of the year, until the animals were brought to market—if they weren't killed first, along with the cowboy. Remaining a cowboy meant doing the same thing year after year, when the only certainty was uncertainty and dust: dust that clogged the nose and throat and dust on the horizon that meant trouble.

The nature of the longhorn was to fight for freedom,

3

which made the job of the cowboy extremely difficult. Freedom may be a cherished American value, but it was always the priority of an animal that would not submit to restraint and had the strength to overpower the cowboy. The hardships they endured together pushed humans and animals to the limit. Both led dangerous lives, and their story was more dramatic than anything experienced by imaginary cowboys. It starts in Texas during that period of history when cowboys were called *vaqueros*.

ONE

Nature's Lovely Miracle

The first cowboys were of Spanish descent, and the methods they developed for controlling cattle were copied by American cowboys. When Spain ruled Texas in the early 1800s, only a few thousand people lived in the area, and the main activity was cattle raising. The ranchers, called *rancheros,* owned large tracts of land where cattle grazed and mixed with other herds on the open range. To separate the animals and move them to new pastures, the rancheros hired men skilled in managing cattle, vaqueros.

Vaqueros originated in Spain, where cattle raising was an important industry, and vaqueros managed cattle

A drawing of early cowboys on a cow hunt.

in Texas and California, which Spain also controlled. Using a rawhide rope called a *reata,* the vaqueros could lasso a galloping steer and bring it to a halt by turning its head. To separate animals, they rode into herds whistling loudly and yelling and then drove the different groups to a new pasture or a ranch.

For mounts, vaqueros preferred wild mustangs, which they roped and then tamed to use as cow ponies. Smaller than most horses, the mustangs could make sharp turns to stay with an animal about to be roped. The vaquero motto was, "Praise the tall, but saddle the small." Vaqueros wore leather chaps to protect their legs against brush and carried pistols to discourage wolves and cougars from preying on the herd. Their ancestors in Spain had polished their skills for hundreds of years, and the vaqueros who were employed in Texas found the work easy. The animals they managed were relatively tame and were confined to a small area in the southern part of the region.

But the cattle business in Texas would soon change entirely because of the appearance of longhorns. These animals were one of nature's great miracles, and they came about quite accidentally after new settlers moved into Texas.

In 1821, Mexico won its independence from Spain and assumed control of Texas and California. At the time, few people lived in Texas, and Mexico feared losing the region to the United States, which might easily overrun it. So the Mexican government allowed Americans to settle in Texas, starting in the early 1820s.

The Americans who came set up their own ranches using black polled beef cattle, a type called Black Angus or Aberdeen Angus. These animals had short legs, short hair, often no horns, and resembled milk cows. They were distinctly different from Mexican cattle, which were larger and more muscular. Originally from Spanish stock, they had long legs, long hair, and sharp horns. The two breeds existed side by side until fate brought them together.

Short-horned cattle.

In 1835, Americans in Texas revolted against Mexican rule, mainly because Mexico had abolished slavery in 1829 and tried to enforce the law in Texas. Mexico and Texas went to war. During the conflict, many ranches were abandoned and the cattle grazed as they pleased. After several months of fighting, the Americans won the war in 1836 and established the Republic of Texas. Now the focus in Texas shifted to farming crops, with slaves doing the work. As a result, the cattle continued to roam free.

The animals found their own food and water, moving and resting without supervision. The herds left the southern part of the state and drifted north and west, feeding on the grasses between the Rio Grande and the upper Panhandle. Since almost no one lived in this part of

7

Texas, the animals had the whole area to themselves.

It was on the plains of west Texas that the two breeds of cattle finally met. Fighting for the right to mate, the Mexican bulls charged the Anglo bulls, gouging their necks with sharp horns, knocking them down, and driving them off. For the next thirty years, after thousands of violent collisions, Mexican cattle mated with Anglo cattle. During the same period, mustangs roamed free and multiplied. The final result was staggering: by 1865, approximately five million cattle and one million mustangs roamed the western half of Texas. Other than numbers, the mustangs hadn't changed much. But the Anglo and Mexican cattle had fashioned themselves into a new breed that was strong, intelligent, and deadly when provoked. Texans invented a name for these animals: longhorns.

A longhorn.

The longhorns stood over six feet high, with long legs and lanky bodies built for speed. They could be any color—black, brown, burnt orange, or all three—with splotches of white in no particular pattern. Their long heads gave them a sinister look, and their mean appearance was bolstered by gigantic horns that could span eight feet from tip to tip. They had survived droughts, blizzards, and wolf attacks by developing tough hides, hard hooves, and attitude. They could walk fifteen miles for a drink of water and make it last for three days. And at the first sign of trouble, they would charge, with twelve hundred pounds of battering-ram muscle, head down and horns up. The Texas rancher Frank Sayer said the longhorn was "fifty times more dangerous than the fiercest buffalo." Another rancher said, "If I had my choice, I would rather face a wounded bear than a longhorn."

The Texans and Mexicans had known about the longhorns for years but had left them alone. The Texans grew cotton and other crops, and Mexicans had reestablished ranches that produced all the beef that was needed in Texas. The longhorns were hard to capture and probably impossible to control. Also, there was no railroad in Texas that might be used to ship them to the big cities in the East. So the longhorns seemed worthless—until the end of the American Civil War in 1865.

By that year a railroad had reached Missouri, and in 1866 it would reach Kansas, allowing for the shipment of western products to eastern markets. If longhorns could be driven north to Kansas and shipped by the railroad, easterners would pay handsomely for the beef, bringing much-needed money to Texas. It sided with the South during the Civil War, and when the South lost and slavery was abolished, the economy of Texas was in ruins. Farms had been abandoned and were overrun with weeds, and with slavery over, money was needed so laborers could be hired to work the crops.

Although Americans craved meat of all kinds, most of their diet consisted of pork, vegetables, and grain because beef was expensive and scarce. But the railroad changed that. Cattle had been driven north before the Civil War, but these early drives ended in failure—those animals had not been strong enough to travel the distance and died on the way. Now, it seemed to some, there was an animal in west Texas that could make the trip. Only mustangs, vaqueros, and a trail route to Kansas were needed—plus the cooperation of the longhorns.

Thus began the era of the American cowboy in 1866, when plans were made to capture longhorns and trail them to Kansas. In Texas the term "cowboy" was used

Nate Love, a famous African American cowboy who had been born into slavery, photographed in 1880. Also known as Deadwood Dick, Love later went on to become a performer and Pullman porter.

A young cowboy, or "greenie."

exclusively to refer to men who caught longhorns and drove them to Kansas. In 1866, most of the cowboys were vaqueros and African Americans. Vaqueros were hired because they had experience with cattle, and some African Americans had worked on ranches in Texas and could ride and rope. Only about a third of the cowboys in 1866 were Anglo, and they followed the lead of the vaqueros and African Americans.

The Anglos were called "greenies" or "green boys." Most of them were farmhands in their late teens or early twenties and many were illiterate. Some became cowboys because they liked the outdoors and were lured by the excitement of working with wild animals. But far more became cowboys because there were few jobs in Texas after the Civil War, and if greenies could ride a horse and shoot a gun, they met the minimum requirements for the job.

After vaqueros and African Americans pioneered the techniques for controlling longhorns, the greenies copied the techniques and took over. They replaced the original cowboys, mostly because it was the only work the Anglos could find. On a typical cattle drive, two-thirds of all the cowboys were new to the job, and most would quit after one drive. This meant that two-thirds were greenies pitted against an animal that took pride in being wild.

From 1866 to 1885, cowboys and longhorns made the trip to Kansas with varying degrees of success. Their trip was called the Long Drive, and it affected countless people and animals. It started in January of each year in west Texas, with cowboys riding hard and firing guns in the air. The first step was to capture some longhorns.

INDIAN COWBOY, MONT.

A greenie. Note the photographer's mark "Indian Cowboy, Mont."

TWO

Brush Poppers and Cactus Bloomers

The ride into west Texas was called the "cow hunt," when the earth shook and the sky turned red from clouds of dust. Conducted in January and February at the start of each trailing season, the cow hunt lasted about six weeks. The first cow hunts were no problem for the longhorns: they just ran away and left the cowboys empty-handed. It took several years to find ways of catching the animals. Typically, a rancher hired fifteen cowboys for a hunt: four or five with experience in capturing longhorns and the rest of them greenies. The cow hunt was different from the "roundup," where tame animals are formed into a herd and moved elsewhere. The cow hunt resembled war, with casualties on both sides.

It was impossible to capture longhorns when they were at full strength, so one technique was to wear them down in what was called the "chase." As cowboys neared an area with a hundred or so longhorns, the longhorns ran, as all wild animals do at the sight of humans. Cowboys gave chase at full gallop and rode alongside the running cattle. As the heavy longhorns pulverized the ground, the riders were hit by chunks of earth and stones sent hurling through the air. They fired pistols to keep the animals running at full speed to wear them down faster. The longhorns had run away from danger before, but gunfire was new to them and must have been truly frightening.

Any animal might charge at a cowboy during the first hour of the chase, when the cattle were still strong. Most often, bulls charged; it was in their nature to fight and they weren't afraid of some guy on a horse. They worked their way to the outside of the pack and tried to slam the cowboys to the ground. To defeat them, the cowboys tried

Hollywood's version of a dusty trail.

to shoot the bulls through the thick part of their horns. If the bullet struck dead center, the pain caused the animal to lose focus and withdraw. But since cowboys fired while riding at full speed, they often missed the horns and hit the head or neck, and the bulls died. Other longhorns died from bullets meant for charging bulls.

After a few hours, the chase slowed to a speedy trot, but that did not mean the longhorns had surrendered. At a slower rate of speed, they could run for two days without stopping or sleeping. Since mustangs were good for only about three hours, the cowboys changed horses often; one of the greenies was designated to bring mounts to the other riders. The switch had to happen fast so the rider could catch up with the chase.

13

At the start of the chase, some longhorns tried to break away from the pack and make their own escape route. Experienced cowboys knew this would happen and watched for it. If an animal made a dash in a different direction, the cowboy tried to lasso the horns and throw the animal to the ground. Dazed from the fall, the "outlaw" usually rejoined the pack. "Outlaw" was the cowboy word for a longhorn that wouldn't obey. Greenies might try to lasso an outlaw or just yell that one was getting away.

The longhorns didn't know where they were going, especially after two or three days of running in unfamiliar terrain. The result was often deadly. To avoid capture, some herds plunged into rivers, where a number of animals, weak and exhausted, drowned. Cowboys and mustangs in the same condition also died in the swift water. Other groups reached the edge of a cliff and those in the lead fell to their death. The rest stopped and broke ranks, some running to the right and some to the left; experienced hands had to decide immediately which group to follow. It was never clear how a chase would end and who would survive. Mustangs broke their legs in potholes and sometimes crushed their riders. A cowboy on the ground was an easy target for a longhorn fighting for freedom.

A trailing stopped at a watering hole.

Most often, the chase ended in stillness on a west Texas prairie. Gasping for breath, with hides soaking in sweat, the longhorns ran until they could run no more. When they slowed and finally stopped, the cowboys prepared to push the cattle into a circular herd. Bulls with reserve strength made a final charge, toppling mustangs and goring their stomachs. The charging bulls were shot; afterward, cowboys rode in slowly and nudged the longhorns with ropes. But at this point, the approach of a mustang was usually enough to get the animals to move into one mass of cattle. They dropped to the ground, and the cowboys then took turns sleeping. After a day or two of rest, the cowboys started the animals on the trip to a ranch in south Texas.

The chase only worked on the open plains of west Texas. A different method was used to capture longhorns in the brush country between the Pecos River and the Rio Grande. From previous raids, the animals had learned to hide in thick brush during the day and graze only at night. To capture the wary cattle, ranchers hired highly experienced cowboys called "brush poppers." They were aided by greenies, who were told to be quiet and not panic.

There were two types of longhorns that were especially tricky for the brush poppers to control: "mossy horns" and "steers." Both were defiant, and the other cattle wouldn't budge until these outlaws were made to submit. Mossy horns were twelve years or older, with moss on their backs and horns. Most had never known captivity, while some had escaped from ranches and returned to brush country. Steers were neutered, runaway males who were strongly belligerent. On the plains, mossy horns and steers could be made to run for three days during the chase, until they were too tired to fight. In brush country, they stood their ground.

With greenies following at a distance, the brush poppers moved quietly against the outlaws. They drove "decoy" herds of tame cattle into the tangle of thickets and cacti. The decoys had a settling effect on the wild

15

animals, and the riders guided the tame animals in at a slow pace so they could gradually mingle. With luck, the decoys moved in and the cattle stayed calm. Not so with mossy horns and steers. When they smelled mustangs, they knew there was trouble. A brush popper wore thick leather chaps, a tough hat, and gloves made of bull hide, all to prepare for the inevitable.

A longhorn today.

Head down, horns up, snorting and bellowing, the mossy horns and steers charged, like bulls in a bullfight. The agile mustangs darted around trees, cacti, and clusters of mesquite to avoid the sharp horns, while greenies hesitated to go farther without directions. If they couldn't see the brush poppers, the greenies could hear them working: the pounding of earth, the crunching of brush, and the cry of an animal whose flesh had been cut by thorns. The cattle became bloody and weak from

16

chasing the riders, but some could pursue the cowboys for hours. Because they became stuck with so many thorns, these animals were called "cactus bloomers."

One method of defeating an outlaw in the brush was to have a second rider approach from behind, lasso the horns, and have the mustang circle a tree for leverage. A clever mossy horn or steer, recognizing the move, would race around the tree and meet the rider on the other side. In this case, the mustang would be gored or the cowboy would cut the rope and run. If the rider could circle the tree with his rope and tie the animal to the tree, it was left there until it became so weak from trying to escape that it gave up and lay down. Once cut free, it would walk away and join the other cattle.

Another maneuver was to approach from behind at a gallop and grab the animal's long tail. After winding the tail around the saddle horn, the rider would have his mount put on a burst of speed and turn sharply. The longhorn would be sent tumbling end over end and sometimes break its neck—an unintended consequence, since cowboys only wanted to stun and disorient outlaws.

Roping the cows.

A herd of longhorn on the plain.

A third method was called "tailing." Again, a rider would approach from behind at full gallop, grab the tail, and, with a sharp jerk, break it. This would also cause the animal to tumble and possibly break its neck. More often, the animal would be in so much pain from the broken tail that it would withdraw to recover. Outlaws that refused to submit were shot, as were charging bulls. And cowboys were in equal jeopardy. A reporter from Refugio County who witnessed a cow hunt in brush country left a chilling account of what could happen to a rider:

> While riding in the thick mesquite, it became necessary to rope a large and powerful steer with long horns, well set for hooking, and sharp as a lance. He fought and fought and would not cooperate. . . . The steer, before he could be thrown, jerked the horse down, the lasso being tied

to the horn of the saddle. The fall of the horse caught the leg of the rider under him. The cowboy struggled to get out from under the horse, but the horse, stunned by the fall, could not get up. The steer, seeing both horse and rider down, turned and charged on them with all his force. With neck bowed, he was ready to strike deep into their vitals with the weapons nature had given him. It was an awful moment. There appeared to be no escape. Some people in such a situation would have been paralyzed—would have lost all presence of mind. But not so with the rider. His hand was instantly on his revolver, and he shot the furious animal through the brain, when the delay of an instant would have been fatal.

The rider in this account may have been a greenie, but more than likely he was an experienced cowboy.

After subduing the mossy horns and steers, the cowboys drove the remaining longhorns out of the brush. Greenies nudged the animals with ropes, and mustangs pushed the cattle into the open. The cattle were formed into a circular herd, with cowboys taking turns sleeping after a full day's work (or sometimes two) without rest. If the mustangs weren't gored, they were stuck with so many thorns that it took hours to remove them while the horses were held down. Brush poppers and greenies could have just as many thorns; their legs could be torn open from horns and vegetation. As both the men and animals rested before the trip to south Texas, the entire scene looked like a battlefield where the fight had ended in a standoff.

The cow hunt occurred at a time when the number of longhorns seemed limitless, and there was little regard for the pain and suffering of animals. The cowboys weren't necessarily cruel by the standards of their time.

They didn't kill longhorns needlessly but did what was required to secure stock. Longhorns were no docile milk cows. They were tough, and the men who captured them were tough—yet with so few experienced hands, it is surprising that the cowboys managed to catch any longhorns at all. Defeated for the moment, the longhorns rested to regain strength for the next round in the fight. This wasn't the rodeo, where animals are outnumbered and overpowered.

After the cow hunt, cowboys prepared to drive the longhorns to south Texas, while the brush poppers stayed behind in west Texas. Four or five experienced hands had to be hired to help the greenies trail the cattle, while longhorns taken in a chase were trailed by the same cowboys who had caught them. The trip to south Texas took about a month. For greenies, it was their first experience in trailing cattle, and for most of the captured longhorns—some had escaped from previous drives—it would be their first experience in being trailed. Once the cattle had rested for a few days, they regained their strength, and they looked at the cowboys with suspicious eyes.

It took at least an hour, and in some cases half a day, to arrange the longhorns in such a way that they might be made to walk in a line in a specific direction. An experienced trail hand named Carr Pickett said the process "was usually successful after two or three tries." Steers and mossy horns, the natural leaders, were roped and dragged to the front of what would become the line of cattle; it took two riders and two ropes to get one of these animals positioned in front. Riders then pushed the other cattle into some sort of line behind them. At first, they were turned every which way, and the goal was to position the longhorns facing the leaders so they might follow them when the line was started. Moving the line took yelling and hitting the animals with ropes. It was a stop-and-go process, with gaps between groups of longhorns, but once they were all walking in a line, they stayed in place—for a little while.

As soon as the longhorns realized they were leaving home, they wanted to run, and the farther they were from home, the more they wanted to run. Every day, and

An orderly cattle drive.

sometimes every hour, a longhorn would bolt for freedom to the plains of west Texas or brush country. Two experienced cowboys stayed with the lead animals. The other experienced hands rode up and down the line of cattle on either side, watching for runaways. Greenies rode close to the cattle to keep them pinched in and walking behind each other.

When an outlaw broke ranks and ran, a seasoned cowboy would rope the animal, throw it to the ground, and then lead it, dazed and stunned, back to the pack. The worst offenders were subdued by "necking," tying the creature by the neck to the neck of a tame longhorn or ox. Bound to another animal by rawhide that didn't stretch, the outlaw tossed its head and tried to gore its partner as the two stumbled along with a greenie riding behind. After a week or so, the longhorn usually lost its will to fight and upon release would fall into line.

When mossy horns and steers ran off, others followed—six, a dozen, and sometimes twenty or more. In such cases, there weren't enough cowboys to capture the runaways and still hold the herd, so the runaways were allowed to go. Experienced hands recognized the steers and mossy horns that they had captured before and never managed to deliver to a ranch in south Texas. West Texas was home, a place of safety where outlaws ruled.

In riding close to the animals, greenies learned to beware of outlaws of another sort: cows with calves. A wild animal will do anything to protect its young, and when a cowboy came too close to a calf, the mother charged. Other cows with calves instinctively joined in. As many as four cows might attack at once, goring a mustang from all sides and the cowboy, too, if he was knocked off his mount. Fighting for others is characteristic of animals that live in a group, and rarely was only one longhorn upset. If a cowboy was being attacked by two cows and a steer, with the steer trying to help or take over, then the rider would be distracted from his watch duties, leaving part of the herd unguarded. That was the signal for another group of longhorns to bolt for freedom.

Cows with calves too young to keep up the pace posed another problem. In the early years, when longhorns were plentiful, cowboys solved this problem by shooting the calves. They were eaten as trail food or just shot and left behind. And if a cow gave birth during the trip to south Texas, the mother would be roped and held to the ground while her newborn was taken away and shot; the mother's tail would be broken as a distraction from her loss.

In later years, more attention was paid to saving the calves. Cowboys carried them across their horses or carted them in a wagon. The males were especially valuable: a

Artist's rendering of cowboys separating calves from their mothers.

full-grown male had more meat than a cow, and males had the stamina needed for the Long Drive. Counting the calves that were saved, an average of 80 percent of the cattle secured in the cow hunt were delivered to south Texas. But it wasn't unusual to lose half of the stock during the trip. Much depended on the number of experienced hands to keep as many cattle captive as possible.

The next phase occurred in March and early April as the herds approached the ranches spread over south Texas. The sound of screaming cattle and the smell of the branding fires were terrifying—even non-outlaws would try to run. But they were outmatched by men from the ranch who rode out to drive the animals into pens, where they were easily roped. Here they would be branded for identification, and it was at this point that two-thirds of the greenies on the cow hunt quit cowboy life. They took

Branding calves.

BRANDING CALVES

their poverty wage of around $30 and went home.

The longhorns were branded to ensure that the right owner would be paid if and when the animal made it to Kansas—the end of the trail. One man would throw a calf to the ground and hold it down while another pressed a hot poker against the animal's hindquarter to burn in a brand. Four men were needed to pin a

Cattle penned up on a Texas ranch.

full-grown longhorn, holding its legs and horns and sitting on the animal until the mark was seared into flesh. At other ranches, longhorns were driven into a corral, a narrow aisle of posts and rails, which kept the animals penned while a brand was applied. It took approximately a week for experienced cowboys, working ten-hour days, to mark the herd.

During branding, smoke from the fires mingled with the odor of sizzling flesh to create a horrible smell. In a drizzling rain, the smell was worse, but the screaming of the cattle never changed. It was deafening. The Texas cowboy S. R. Cooper said, "You would have to holler to make a man hear you that was right next to you, and before you got your mouth shut again, it and your throat would be filled with dust and smoke from the burning hair." Castration of young bulls was also done on the ranch, where most were kept for fattening until they were strong enough to be trailed north.

This was the pattern of the first phase of the Long Drive: six weeks of warfare in west Texas, resistance on the trip from home, then branding and castration, followed by greenies returning to farms and a new batch of greenies hired for the trip to Kansas. Unaware that they would become legendary figures, most cowboys left no record of the cow hunt, branding, and the like; many couldn't write, either. The accounts that were written came from men who enjoyed the work year after year and took the time to describe it.

Rocky Reagan left one of the most informative accounts, from the starting point in west Texas to a ranch in south Texas. A brush popper in the 1860s, Reagan was moving into a thicket when . . .

. . . suddenly, I heard a noise in the brush, almost back of me. I looked. There charging out of it, his head raised like a buck deer's and the coarse hair on his back standing up, came a big old red-roan steer. . . . When he saw men, he wheeled back into cover. He had long been wanted. The horse I was riding was about run down. It happened that our cook had come out with us that day, and his horse was fresh. It didn't take a minute for us to change saddles. I had an idea where the old roan had gone, and I hit his trail on the run. . . .

In a thicket of white brush I got close enough to throw my rope and caught him by only one horn. At the feel of the rope, instead of breaking loose, as he could have done very easily, he wheeled like a cutting horse and rammed one of his sharp horns into the breast of my mount. The horn went in six or eight inches. The horse stood there trembling. Maybe I was trembling too. For what seemed like a good while the steer remained in his tracks, working—gouging—his horn deeper into the horse. Then he gave a jerk, turned, and left. I was helpless, without any sort of gun. The horse died.

Six months later we jumped that same steer about eight miles from where he had hooked my horse. I roped him and the rope broke. A Mexican then roped him and we tied him to a tree. The next day I sent this Mexican and another hand with a lead ox to bring the outlaw in. When they got to the tree, they found the steer had broken the tying rope and fled. . . .

[The next winter] four of my men jumped the old roan and took after him. Right at the Nueces River one of them roped him. He went to fighting, and while the rider was unfastening the rope from his saddlehorn, the steer killed his horse. Meantime the other three boys had come up and were roping at him. One of them caught him, but when Old Roan raked his horse, he turned him loose. The steer made for a third man and snagged his horse's hip.

Old Roan now had one dead horse and two wounded ones to his credit, all in a pile. And he had two ropes dragging from his head. He swam the river and on the other side stopped in a drift. He stood there awhile, shaking his head, trembling with rage, and then he stepped back into the deep water and swam out by the four men who had chased him. The man on the one untouched horse did not have the nerve to tie into him. I did not blame him. I would not have tackled that steer on a tired horse for a carload of polo ponies.

That winter passed and spring came and nobody had seen hoof or hair of the roan outlaw. Then one day, back in the Jack West pasture, a Mexican and I jumped him in a thicket. He was no longer dragging the ropes that had been left on him. We twined him, threw him down, and tied him doubly fast to a strong mesquite. We went to camp, brought out the best lead ox we had, necked the two together, and put the pair in a bunch of steers. . . .

The roan came along until he was within sight of the ranch. Then he stopped, refused to budge an inch further. For half an hour or so the ox worked him around—or, rather, worked around him—trying to coax and drag him. Finally the ox decided to rest a while himself and lay down. The roan stood there in a clearing looking at the ranch. Directly he dropped dead. I think he was dead before his body hit the ground.

Cattle like these were wise to the movements of men. . . . I have heard of horses starving to death because of an allegiance to a plot of ground. The allegiance of a genuine outlaw is to whatever cover he can find anywhere that will preserve his liberty.

FOUR

The Outfit Moves Out, Scientifically

Dinnertime on the
Chisholm Trail.

The next phase of the journey was moving the herds to Kansas. The trail route north to Kansas kept changing as the railroad reached different towns and longhorns were shipped from different areas in the state. But most longhorns were driven north on the Chisholm Trail. It was a wide path of dirt that started at San Antonio in south Texas, crossed through the Indian Territory, and ended in central Kansas. On average, about two thousand cowboys trailed 300,000 longhorns in a typical year. It was the largest forced migration of animals in American history, and the men who accomplished the feat never knew what the next day might bring.

Chaos often characterized the first week of the drive, when the herd was "trail broken." In the wild, longhorns had three positions: lying down (for sleeping), standing (for eating), and running (to avoid danger). They had to learn to walk for twelve hours a day in an orderly way, along with ranch cattle and animals from different groups in west Texas. Having undergone branding and confinement at a ranch for up to a month, they were not always willing to walk in a line.

There were two ways of getting the cattle adjusted to the routine of walking. They could be trailed at a slow pace for only three hours at a time; or they could be pushed to walk fast all day to build stamina and keep them out of trouble. Whatever the approach, mossy horns and steers knew that something was wrong. When so many cattle were pushed together and made to walk, they sensed a bad situation and knew it was time to get out.

Plodding along, with their eyes shifting back and forth, they would bolt from the herd and run as fast as they could for any place where they might be free. When a cowboy gave chase, unguarded longhorns made a run for it, having learned the procedure on the trip from west Texas. Others with no experience in escaping also ran: for example, beeves, steers from four to six years old who

The Chisholm Trail today.

had been raised on a ranch and had never known freedom. It was in their nature to be free, and being under the control of humans for years hadn't changed that.

If more than a hundred longhorns were on the loose—as happened frequently—then the drive was stopped until order was restored by tailing and necking the outlaws. Other methods of control were also used to restrain the herd.

Outlaws that wouldn't obey—even after tailing and necking—had their eyes sewn shut with strips of buckskin so they couldn't see where to run.

Captured longhorns considered mustangs to be their enemies and didn't like it when the horses drew near to keep the herd in a line. When a longhorn gored a mustang, cowboys tied the outlaw's head to its own front leg so it couldn't maneuver quickly for another charge.

Longhorns that always wanted to run had their hamstrings cut or had dirt and tobacco juice rubbed in their eyes to blind them and break their will.

Sometimes it was considered necessary to cut a hole through the animal's nose and insert a rope that was jerked to get it to obey. Others had their horns chopped off with an ax, causing tremendous pain and compliance. Longhorns that wouldn't submit, despite these efforts, were shot and eaten as trail food. After a week or so of such treatment, the outlaws were broken and the herd accepted the routine.

Most of the first drives ended in failure since so many longhorns died. So changes were made to make the drives more profitable. It was learned that herds of about two thousand cattle could easily become unprofitable if too many animals died before reaching Kansas. Other drives made it clear that herds of about four thousand required too much pasturage along the trail and were too hard to control. About three thousand longhorns became the usual number for a herd, and in an average year, one hundred herds of three thousand cattle each headed for Kansas in March and April, when prairie grass was lush.

The Long Drive became a science, besides a business, with its own vocabulary—and on paper, at least, it looked as though it could work.

An "outfit" included everything needed to move the cattle on the Long Drive. A typical outfit had eighteen men and about one hundred mustangs. The "trail boss" controlled all operations of the outfit: he decided where to cross rivers, when to stop the drive each day, and how long the cattle should rest. The trail boss was an experienced cowboy who could be trusted to deliver as many cattle as possible. He rode miles ahead of the herd three or four times each day to check rivers and grazing areas and to look for trouble. Because the men under him sometimes got into fights with one another, or sometimes drank too much alcohol, the trail boss tended to be a large man who was good with his fists. And he could be trusted to stay sober. According to the trail boss Bill Poage:

> He has as many duties as the captain of a steamboat. He must assign each man to his proper duty. He must be first up in the morning to see that there is water ahead and he must count the cattle at intervals to see that none have been lost. He must settle all difficulties among his men and make sure that none are too drunk to ride.

A trail boss was paid $125 a month—a high salary for the

An advertisement for cattlemen.

A cowboy at the start of a cattle drive.

1860s and 1870s and more than most skilled workers made.

The cook was the second highest paid member, at $75 a month. Most cooks were former cowboys who had become too old for that work or who were disabled and could no longer ride. The cook transported all of his supplies in a "chuck wagon" and prepared three meals a day for the outfit. His food was an often discussed subject. It was said that some cooks made "six-shooter" coffee every morning: it was so strong that it could probably float a pistol. If meals were overcooked or repeated for days, the men complained constantly—but rarely to the cook. Cooks were known to be cranky and would shortchange critics with small biscuits and the last of the beans stuck to the bottom of the pot. Many were heavy drinkers, too. Greenies were quick to learn the first rule of the trail: "Only a fool argues with a skunk, a mule, or a cook."

The cowboy in charge of the horses was called the "wrangler." He was usually "a fryin' size young fellow jus' learnin' to be a cowboy," one trail boss said. Most were fifteen or sixteen years old, and they managed the mustangs, which were so crucial to the drive.

During the day, the wrangler herded the mustangs at some distance from the cattle; he brought fresh mounts to the cowboys every four hours. When the herd stopped for lunch and dinner, he helped the cook by gathering "cow chips" (dried cow droppings) for the fire and by pouring coffee. At night, he kept the horses in a *remuda,* a makeshift pen where the animals were encircled with ropes tied to posts. He tried to keep them away from woods and canyons, where a horse might try to escape. Some mustangs still had a streak of wildness and would run if given the chance, in which case the wrangler was ridiculed for it. He was the butt of many jokes, as was the "nighthawk," or night wrangler, who was just below the wrangler in status. The nighthawk brought horses to cowboys on night patrol and generally did whatever anyone told him to do.

Apart from the cook and the trail boss, an average outfit had only four experienced cowboys. The two most experienced hands took positions at the front of the herd, one on the right and one on the left. They were called

WRANGLER REMUDA CHUCK WAGON

DRAG FLANK SWING POINT TRAIL BOSS

DRAG

DRAG FLANK SWING POINT

"pointers" or "point men," and they watched out for trouble: rattlesnakes, wild longhorns that might charge, and any change in the ground that might cause a problem for the cattle—such as gopher holes, shale, or stones that could lodge in hooves.

Pointers let the front of the herd spread out to fifty feet

The formation of cowboys around the herd.

35

across, but steers actually led the herd. The biggest steers forced their way to the front and assumed the role of leaders, as if they were still in charge. Jim Flood, an experienced pointer, put it this way: "The secret to trailing wild cattle is to never let them know they are under restraint. Let everything that is done be done naturally and voluntarily by the cattle."

Because there wasn't much dust in front of the herd, pointers inhaled less dust than other trail hands. But if the herd was moving in such a way that one man was getting more dust than the other, then the pointers switched positions every day so they would be equally dirty. The status of a cowboy was determined by dust and dirt: the dirtier his clothing, the lower his status.

The next pair of cowboys were the "swing men." They had experience in turning a herd to avoid obstacles and rocky terrain. Like pointers, swing men had once been greenies who had stayed with the work and moved up in status. Because they hoped to be point men someday but for now had to take orders from them, there was usually friction between pointers and swing men. "They think they know it all," said the swing man Cody Applegate, "and they shout out orders as if we can't see where the trail is heading." Swing men rode about ten feet behind the lead steers and inhaled more dust than pointers.

Next in line were three pairs of men called "flankers." They were greenies; they kept the herd stretched back in a line over half a mile long to avoid overheating. Their other job was to keep the animals walking at a steady pace—rather than trotting, which meant they'd be ready to run. If a flanker spotted a trotter, he rode into the herd and yanked the animal's tail to slow it down. Necking controlled longhorns who still had a tendency to run.

The heavy longhorns created a cloud of dirt that covered the herd. Because of this, swing men and flankers changed position each day. Swing men switched sides every day, while the first flanker on the right moved to the left and on the next day moved to the second row of flankers and so on, until he was back in his original

A cattle drive shown from the back, featuring the "drag riders."

position. The rotation ensured that all flankers were equally dirty, and no cowboy could pick a fight over how he looked at the end of the day.

Last in status were the "drag riders," who were the greenest of the greenies—they could stay on a horse and that was about all. Three or four drag riders followed the herd and they were always encased in dirt. They didn't change positions because wherever they were they were still behind the herd—after a few hours, they were barely recognizable. Drag riders pushed yearlings and weaker cattle to keep up. Besides dirt, they breathed in the full smell of cattle droppings. The cowboy J. L. McCaleb said this was the best place to learn cusswords.

All trail hands, from pointers to drag riders, were paid the same wages by ranchers: $25 to $40 a month. The fact that experienced cowboys were paid the same as greenies indicates that ranchers had low regard for the job—and that their goal for a cattle drive was maximum profit for themselves.

If all went well, a good day would be marked by

boredom, dirt, and grogginess from lack of sleep. Every cowboy rode night patrol to watch for wolves or any threat to the herd. They rode in two-hour shifts between 8 P.M. and 4 A.M. Greenies got the worst time slot, from midnight to 2 A.M., which meant they got four hours of sleep at most. Usually, four men rode in a shift, but if the herd was threatened or spooked—for example, by lightning—the entire outfit worked throughout the night, and sometimes two nights, without sleep. It was said that a cowboy learned to do his sleeping in the winter.

Regardless of what happened during the night, the day started at 4 A.M. with the rattling of pots and pans and with cowboys turning under their blankets to find level ground that might give them more sleep. Within a half hour or so, the cook would yell, "Roll out! Come an' get it!" Or . . .

A "nighthawk" guarding the herd.

Bacon in the pan,
Coffee in the pot!
Get up an' get it—
Get it while it's hot!

It seemed to some cowboys that the cook enjoyed ending their sleep as soon as possible. But he was only doing his job, and the men had to start eating before the sun was fully up.

Dinnertime, including the chuck wagon. Note the remuda in the background.

By five o'clock the trail boss was gone, and the men were eating biscuits dipped in molasses, potatoes boiled in vinegar, or a steak from an animal that hadn't been able to keep up. After downing a last cup of coffee, each man slung his saddle over a shoulder and headed for the remuda to pick a horse for the morning. Once mounted, they surrounded the cattle and rode in, causing most of the longhorns to stand up. Then the cowboys pinched the herd into a makeshift line. The trail boss returned to shout "Move 'em out!" or swearwords if the herd wasn't quite ready for the day. Pointers nudged the lead steers to get them walking, swing men fell into line, greenies took new positions as flankers, and drag riders tied kerchiefs across their faces. The last cowboys on night watch were eating when the herd moved out. After breakfast, they bedded down for a few hours before catching up with the herd.

By ten o'clock the flankers and drag riders were covered in dirt, and if it was raining, the dirt had turned to mud. Saddle blisters began to ache and riders itched from insect bites gotten overnight. After six hours on the trail, the drive was stopped for the noon meal, during which the cattle fed on pasturage and dozed. Then, after the noon meal, the herd was brought to its feet for another six-hour march, but this time in heat that could be higher than one hundred degrees.

As with the morning march, the bellowing of three thousand longhorns and the pounding of the earth made normal talk impossible. Communication was done by hand and arm signals: these might indicate "Moving left," for example, or "Slow the herd" (for a hazard or a change in terrain). Because the line of cattle could be more than half a mile long, each man rode alone and didn't say more than a few words during the entire day.

Although the ideal was six hours on the trail in the morning and six hours in the afternoon, it was difficult to achieve. The distance from San Antonio to central Kansas was about six hundred miles, and a typical herd covered about fifteen miles a day—if they were lucky. Often they didn't get nearly that far on a given day.

To stay awake for twelve hours on a horse—if the ideal was accomplished—cowboys rubbed tobacco juice in their eyes and mumbled songs:

> *Billy was a bad man,*
> *And carried a big gun.*
> *He was always after Greasers,*
> *And kept 'em on the run.*
> *He shot two in the morning,*
> *For to make his morning meal.*
> *And if a man should sass him,*
> *He was shore to feel his steel.*

And

> *Our cook is a very dirty man—*
> *Sail away for the Rio Grande—*
> *He cooks the food as dirty as he can—*
> *Sail away for the Rio Grande.*

"Greaser" was a slang word for Mexicans, and many cowboy songs included racist names for other nonwhite groups. In their attitude toward nonwhites, cowboys were like many others during their time. But the notable fact about their songs is that most contained so much profanity that they can't be repeated.

A cowboy usually had one change of clothing that had to last for four months. When possible, he bathed in

streams, washed his clothes, and changed every few days. To rid their clothing of lice, cowboys placed their shirts and pants on anthills until the ants carried off the lice. Then they washed the clothes with suds from yucca roots and let the suds dry to kill the ants.

Packing up in the morning before the start of the day's drive.

For toilet paper, they used pages from mail-order catalogs. For drinking water, they often had to rely on streams tainted with alkali and other pollutants that gave them diarrhea. Most didn't shave or cut their hair during the Long Drive; they didn't bother to keep too clean because it wasn't possible to stay clean. And it wasn't possible to keep their teeth clean and free of rot, either. There was a joke that cowboys told about their life with the longhorns. A child asked, "Ma, do cowboys eat grass?" and was told, "No, dear, they're partly human."

The best part of a cowboy's day came after the evening meal, around 7 P.M., when the men played poker, smoked tobacco, and told stories of wonder and woe. Sometimes the talk was about real people and events: how Bill Johnson's horse pitched him into a branding fire or how Missouri Pete got so mad at his trail boss that he shot off his hat and quit the outfit, as some cowboys did along the way.

But more often, unsuspecting greenies listened to exaggerated tales called "windies." In one of these, for example, a cowboy faced certain death, only to save

Cowboys winding down for the night.

himself in a surprising way. If a greenie hung on every word, the others tried to hold their laughter until the greenie caught on and realized the story wasn't true. And greenies fell prey to "circular stories," where a cowboy would relate a series of incidents along the trail, recall the same incidents in the same order, and then start again for the third time. When the greenie finally looked puzzled, the others broke into laughter.

After such fun and swigs of whiskey, someone would start singing the most popular song on the Chisholm Trail, and another would pick it up and add more stanzas of profanity. "The Old Chisholm Trail" always started the same way, but otherwise the rest of it just rhymed:

> *Come along, boys, and listen to my tale:*
> *I'll tell you of my troubles on the Old Chisholm Trail.*
> *Come a-ti-yi-yippy, yippy-yay, yippy-yay,*
> *Come a-ti-yi-yippy-yay.*

For many cowboys, their troubles began with rivers. To reach Kansas, an outfit had to cross six major rivers—the Colorado, Brazos, Red, Canadian, Cimarron, and Arkansas—in the spring, at the exact time when they were at flood stage. Boredom ended and chaos reigned when a herd reached its first river.

Longhorns had crossed rivers in west Texas by themselves and had survived for thirty years. They crossed where the river was shallow and the bottom firm, avoiding deep water and swift current. They could swim if they had to, but they were too heavy to swim against a strong current, unless they had to swim for only twenty feet or so. But the rivers they faced on the way to Kansas were from a quarter- to a half-mile wide, deep, and fast. Because a hundred herds were trailed each year, each herd had to keep moving to avoid a traffic jam. A trail boss had two days at most to pick the best spot for crossing a river, even if there was no good spot available.

Crossings that ended in death followed a similar pattern. Pointers and swing men would drag the lead steers into the river while greenies pushed the others to follow. If the current swept away the lead steers, the rest of the herd stopped in midstream. The herd, having lost its leaders, became confused and didn't know which way to go. The end result was that the animals began circling, creating a "mill"—a large swarm of cattle swimming in a circle in the middle of a river. The mill wasn't stationary but was pushed downriver by the current as cowboys tried to gain control and the trail boss screamed orders.

Pointers and swing men tried to grab the horns of animals and pull them in the right direction. Greenies tried to keep the cattle bunched together. The men struggled to stay on their horses; the unlucky ones were toppled by the large horns of the cattle and swept away, drowning with their mounts. The mill might last all day and escalate into several swarms of circling cattle, like pinwheels banging into each other. And it might take ten

Hollywood's image of a herd crossing the Red River. From the film *Red River*.

miles of drifting downriver to complete the crossing. The most desperate time was just before nightfall. The outfit worked frantically to complete the crossing because it was suicidal to ride next to longhorns in a mill in complete darkness.

Of the six major rivers crossed on the Chisholm Trail, the Red River was the most dangerous. Storms upstream could make the river rise suddenly, sometimes while a herd was crossing, and swarms of hornets on its banks made the crossing painful. When their nests were

An actual river crossing.

disturbed, the hornets dive-bombed everything that moved until the intruders were miles from the water. If the hornets hit longhorns in midstream, it was impossible to control the herd. The cattle turned in every direction, not knowing which way to go to avoid the stinging. Neither did the greenies. The Red River was rarely crossed without fatalities, especially when it was dangerously wide and herds became backed up for miles.

In the spring of 1871, the Red River flooded so far over its banks that it was a mile wide. Twenty outfits and sixty thousand cattle were stalled, with the herds close to one another. On the trail, the herds were usually spaced from twenty to fifty miles apart so that mossy horns and steers from one herd had no opportunity to challenge the leaders of another herd.

The herds stalled at the Red River were less than a hundred feet apart, and the leaders regularly charged those of other herds. Cowboys worked without sleep for days to separate the cattle, but the animals only became more rebellious; their pasturage was gone, and they were hungry. Trail bosses blamed each other for the mess, while cowboys had fistfights over name-calling, sometimes while drunk. Meanwhile, Mark Withers, a seasoned cowboy, said, "The litter of heavy brush and broken trees sweeping down the river gave you the feeling that, for hundreds of miles, everything that grew had been plucked out by the roots and sent swirling and bobbing down." Another rider said that the crying and bellowing of sixty thousand cattle "was just as frightening as the sound of the raging water."

The situation grew worse with every passing day. After weeks of waiting, and with the food gone, the rain only got heavier, making the river higher and faster. The first in line to cross the river was an all-Mexican outfit, which finally made the attempt out of desperation. When sixty steers and a vaquero tested the current, the longhorns were swept downstream as soon as they entered the river. Then a submerged log shot to the surface and unseated the vaquero. As he and his horse were carried away, a second vaquero rode in to the rescue. Both men drowned, along with their horses and fifty-two longhorns.

The next herd in line entered the river, and then the next, and the next; the bosses didn't want to lose their place in line. Herds were driven in by gunfire. The Red River became a sea of bobbing heads—longhorns and mustangs—with riders up to their shoulders in water. Six thousand longhorns, ten cowboys, and sixty mustangs drowned.

The rivers carried away wagons, saddles, blankets, and food as cattle were driven into swift water to keep pace with the traffic on the Chisholm Trail. A boss could easily lose a hundred longhorns to rivers big and small; if he wasn't careful, he could lose five hundred or more. The record may have been set at the Canadian River in 1873. It was over its banks and a half-mile wide when pointers taunted a boss for being too cautious. Telling the others to stay back, he led the herd in himself—and 850 longhorns drowned, along with the boss. When trail hands recovered his body downstream, they found a letter in his pocket from his wife. In it, she begged him not to cross rivers when they were flooded.

A flooded river offered an additional challenge: banks of soft mud and quicksand that sucked longhorns down to their bellies. The best spot to cross a river was a place with a firm bank, of course, but that didn't solve the problem of the bank on the other side of the river. And if the cattle were in a mill and drifting downstream, they might exit anywhere, into mud or deadly quicksand. An outfit could be bogged down for three days because of riverbanks. Everyone worked without sleep until the longhorns were dug out.

The experience of George Duffield's herd was fairly typical. On the second week of his drive in 1866, the Brazos River swallowed up ten saddles, several blankets, and miscellaneous supplies. At the Red River crossing, one trail hand and fourteen cattle drowned. Before his outfit crossed the Canadian, Duffield wrote in his diary, "No progress. We dug cattle out of the mud all day. We hauled cattle out with oxen and worked through the night using torches so we could see." The cattle sank again at the Arkansas River: nine steers were lost. They were buried to their necks in quicksand and couldn't be dislodged. They were left to die.

After a month on the trail, the longhorns and the outfit looked like refugees from a war. The cattle were caked in mud and cut from river crossings, and if they'd had their tail broken for some offense, it hung limp and was usually covered with flies. Some still had their eyes sewn shut,

Artist's rendering of digging out a longhorn.

and others were blinded by more douses of tobacco juice, because they had tried to run or wouldn't enter a river. Beeves that had been hobbled walked with a jerky motion, and some longhorns had their heads tied to a leg, having recently tried to gore a mustang. The mustangs were thin, with their bones beginning to show; their bodies ached from saddle sores and sore hooves.

If a cowboy had hired on because of his sense of adventure, he was, by now, questioning his decision. His clothing was soiled and torn, and his face was burned from the heat of the cattle. Permanent boils and sores had formed on his rear end, so he rode in his saddle slightly off center. His hands were coated with axle grease to cover cuts, which came from holding the reins so tightly during river crossings, and he might have a

49

broken arm or cracked rib—from a longhorn or from a fight with another cowboy. But the drive had barely started. Cowboys and longhorns had yet to see all of the troubles waiting for them on the Old Chisholm Trail.

SIX

"That Cloud of Dust on the Horizon"

While they lived outdoors for four months, cowboys encountered other forms of life that were hungry, curious, or protective of their homes. Snakes, scorpions, tarantulas, lizards, and beetles with pincers might startle the cowboys under their blankets at night. Near rivers, cowboys slept under tarps to hide from swarms of mosquitoes—but there was no protection from stinging ants if a cowboy picked the wrong spot to bed down.

The weather, of course, had a crucial effect on their lives. Besides the sun's relentless heat, rainstorms, and lightning strikes, the wind could blow so hard that it was difficult to stay on a horse. At other times hailstones pummeled the cowboys, causing horses to throw their riders and run for cover. On a perfect day, nature was a friend, and the only worry was "that cloud of dust on the horizon" moving toward the herd—a phrase that trail bosses and pointers must have repeated a thousand times—in other words, trouble.

During the Texas part of the trip, the cloud of dust could mean "cattle rustlers," a general term meaning cattle thieves, horse thieves, and all-around thieves. Cattle rustlers thrived in Texas with the Long Drive, which wasn't surprising.

After winning independence from Mexico, Texas became an independent republic that wasn't too good at enforcing the law because there were too many lawbreakers. The laws of the United States did not apply in Texas, and the region became a haven for those fleeing prosecution for crimes committed in the United States. Thieves, murderers, and bad guys in general moved to Texas, where crime continued to be their way of life. Lawlessness was so bad that a special unit, the Texas Rangers, was created to arrest criminals. But the size of

51

Texas and its wide-open spaces made the capture of criminals difficult.

After Texas became a state in 1846, it continued its old ways. It led the nation in the number of citizens who took the law into their own hands to punish criminals, in some cases by hanging. Many of those who performed the hangings went unpunished, even though they had committed a crime.

So Texas, already known for lawlessness, fell on hard economic times after the Civil War. Suddenly, cattle rustling became common—longhorns were worth stealing.

Some former cowboys became cattle rustlers, such as Missouri Pete (who had shot off his boss's hat): there was more money in stealing cattle than in being a cowboy. On the other hand, some cowboys were former rustlers; it was the rule of the trail not to ask a man his last name or too much about his background. The thieves who became cowboys did so either because they had failed at rustling or because they didn't want to risk the penalty if caught: death by hanging.

Texans usually headed the gangs of rustlers, which included men wanted in other states. The Texans knew the route of the trail and how and where to sell stolen longhorns. The rustlers sold the cattle to ranchers in south Texas, along with mustangs, saddles, and guns. They kept the trail bosses' money for replacing equipment, and if the boss had the outfit's pay of around $3,000, the thieves took it, too. The buyers in south Texas, or men working for them, altered the brands and hired a new outfit for a drive. A longhorn that made part of the trip two or three times must have wondered if the strange creatures on horses knew what they were doing. Cowards that they were, the rustlers never tried to match wits with longhorns in west Texas, only those on a drive.

On a drive in 1874, Jack Fabin's outfit was hit by rustlers. They outnumbered his men by five and they approached

Artist's rendering of rustlers.

at a gallop with pistols drawn. The pointers and swing men had seen it before—they drew rifles on the gang as it came within range. Greenies followed with six-shooters, but most didn't have a clue of what might happen. Poised at the front of the herd, Fabin fired warning shots in the air. The rustlers opened fire, and the outfit answered back. Bullets flew for about ten seconds, the average time for this type of confrontation. The rustlers turned and fled, and the only casualty was a mustang that was shot from under a greenie, who stayed pinned until the conflict was over.

The head-on approach worked best when no guns were drawn and rustlers simply blocked the boss and the herd, meaning that they wanted cattle but not necessarily a gunfight. This was more typical than a shoot-out—but if rustlers demanded too many longhorns, the boss might go for his gun. It all depended on the boss and the situation: how many cattle had already been lost, the

53

strength of the opposition, and how much faith the boss had in the greenies to shoot and not run.

Twenty longhorns was the typical price for proceeding, and a shrewd boss used the occasion to dump troublemakers: outlaws still refusing to obey. Although cowboys and rustlers died in shoot-outs, and rustlers ended some drives, the give-and-take approach made it more like a business. If all they could get was ten longhorns, the rustlers could hit the next outfit—and the next after that—before herding the cattle south. In standoffs between rustlers and cowboys, the difference between greenies and the boss was glaring: greenies were scared. The boss stayed calm and relied on his experience to overcome another bump in the Chisholm Trail.

Hollywood's version of a standoff between Native Americans and cattlemen. From the film *The Cowboys.*

After crossing the Red River, the cloud of dust on the horizon could mean Native Americans. During the 1830s, scores of Native American tribes living in the East were forced to give up their land when they refused to accept the white man's law. They were prohibited from owning land as a tribe, as they always had, and they were given a choice: to accept 320 acres of land each or leave. It really wasn't a choice—and most left.

They were given land in the Indian Territory, much of which was arid and unsuitable for farming. Among the first to arrive were the Five Civilized Tribes: the Cherokees, Chickasaws, Choctaws, Creeks, and Seminoles, although some Seminoles stayed behind and fought the United States for years. The tribes in the East were pushed off land that they had occupied for eight thousand years.

The displaced natives made the best of the situation, farming, hunting, and gathering food—and then they were overrun by Texas cattle. Although the United States government had promised that Native Americans would be protected in the Indian Territory from any white intrusion, it did nothing to stop the cattle drives.

In the eastern part of the Indian Territory on the Shawnee Trail, the cattle scared away deer and trampled crops. In retaliation, the Native Americans attacked the herds for meat—but more often, like the rustlers, they stopped herds and demanded cattle before the herd was allowed to proceed. Twenty longhorns was the average and it was called a "tribute," a gesture of respect. Eventually, the natives in the eastern part of the Territory enacted laws requiring a toll for passage through their land: ten cents per longhorn, plus a fee for grazing.

The game of cowboys and Indians was played for real on the Chisholm Trail, which cut through the lands of the Comanches, Apaches, and Osages. Fed up with most things white—including lies—these Native Americans outnumbered cowboys and were mounted and armed. When they confronted an outfit, it wasn't playtime. A hundred or more warriors would charge straight on,

Grave marker of twenty-two-year-old William Cohron, a boss herder shot dead by one of his men who didn't want to follow an order. The murderer was pursued by two cowboys, who eventually caught and shot him.

overrunning a herd and killing all trail hands. The cowboys could win when evenly matched, but it was no cause for celebration. Even in victory, there were casualties—dead men, longhorns, and mustangs.

Greenies grew up fast in the Indian Territory. Shooting and being shot at, hearing of complete outfits being wiped out, and seeing graves with simple headstones reading KILLED BY INDIANS—this wasn't what a greenie expected, and it fueled a hatred of Indians. Most of the greenies didn't know about the Indian removal of the 1830s and didn't care about the effect of longhorns on farming and hunting. All they knew was that Indians were killing whites, and they viewed Indians as "savages." That was already the attitude of many experienced cowboys. In short, they shared the attitude of the majority of American whites during this time.

The most blood was shed in the early years of the Long Drive. In 1866, two greenies rode off to subdue outlaws just south of the Canadian River; they were later found knifed to death and scalped. In 1867, Jim Dobie's outfit was pinned down by Osages; four trail hands were killed and a third of the herd was lost. Frank Love recalled what happened when his outfit was stopped by four hundred Comanches in 1868: "They made us give them a hundred head. There were three or four herds going through, but the cowboy force did not exceed fifty men. We were too weak to hold the herds and fight a force which so greatly outnumbered ours. Under the circumstances, it was better to compromise."

Although Native Americans killed more cowboys than rustlers did, they also used the give-and-take approach. A boss might lose a hundred head in negotiating through the Indian Territory. But he would easily lose a thousand if the outfit showed weakness.

Dust on the horizon in the Indian Territory might mean something else just as serious—buffalo.

At one time, fifty million buffalo roamed the plains

A buffalo herd.

from Texas to North Dakota. The Plains Indians—the Sioux, for example—had relied on the buffalo to live for more than ten thousand years, but the U.S. government viewed the Plains Indians as people who were in the way, and it devised a solution to the problem. As one army officer said, "Kill the buffalo and you've killed the Plains Indians."

The government hired buffalo hunters to kill millions of the animals, some shooting hundreds a day from railroad cars. Some, like William F. Cody—known as "Buffalo Bill"—gained fame and fortune for such deeds. Although whites also hunted buffalo for hides and meat, most of the animals were shot and left to rot as a way of subduing the Plains Indians. It worked. In time they had little to eat and were forced onto reservations.

At the time of the Long Drive, only a few million buffalo remained and the Chisholm Trail cut through some of their grazing area, resulting in the loss of more buffalo. Longhorns and buffalo disliked one another. When buffalo spotted longhorns, they often charged, and longhorns charged back. As the groups became mixed and the losers were gored to the ground, the herd could turn into a dozen mills, longhorns circling buffalo and racing in for a goring and buffalo circling longhorns and trying to topple them.

Experienced cowboys, in this case those experienced with mustangs, rode in and shot the buffalo. But when a

The infamous William F. "Buffalo Bill" Cody.

greenie tried it, he discovered that his mount wouldn't always obey. Mustangs didn't like buffalo, either, and it took skill and experience to get the horses to challenge buffalo. Before captivity, both longhorns and mustangs ran to escape buffalo. Now under the control of humans, they were made to fight battles that cost them their lives. Cowboys died, too.

The cloud of dust at the Kansas border announced the presence of farmers, ranchers, and guards standing shoulder to shoulder, like an army ready to stop an invasion. Farmers were less than happy when herds knocked down fences and ate crops. Kansas ranchers raised their own cattle and didn't want competition from Texans. More important, by 1867 Kansas and six other states had laws prohibiting Texas cattle from crossing their borders. The longhorns were barred because they carried a tick that infected other cattle with what was called "Texas fever" or "Spanish fever." The tick killed thousands of cattle in Kansas, Colorado, Missouri, Nebraska, Ohio, Illinois, and Kentucky, while the longhorns were immune to the disease. The immunity was developed in west Texas and it had served the longhorns well, until the Long Drive.

A barricade of logs and brush across the Chisholm Trail stopped many herds just south of the Kansas border. Rifles and shotguns rested on the structure. If required, they would be fired to keep the hated longhorns out.

When stopped, the cattle had to stay back in the Indian Territory, where an entire herd might die. The cattle used up pasturage and became thin and weakened while cowboys from different outfits fought gunfights over grazing areas. A stationary herd was a tempting target for any buffalo passing by, and if the longhorns had been stuck for too long, they might lack the strength to fight back. During blizzards in the Indian Territory, animals froze to death, and prairie fires killed thousands of longhorns. In the winter of 1867, forty thousand longhorns died in the Indian Territory, unable to get past the guards at the Kansas border.

An experienced boss trailed around the barricades and slipped into Kansas undetected. If his herd was eventually spotted, bullets flew. Occasionally, cowboys were hit—but the bullets were meant for longhorns, which were shot by the thousands in Kansas. Other longhorns were captured or killed by "jayhawkers," gangs of thieves who shot cattle or stole them, on the pretext that they were protecting Kansas from Texas fever.

The warfare in Kansas never stopped, even after a compromise was reached. After a few years, longhorns were allowed to enter Kansas if they had been "wintered" in the Indian Territory—that is, if they had spent a winter in the Territory, where the tick they carried had been killed by the cold temperature. But soon false certificates claiming that longhorns had been wintered were

KANSAS REGULATIONS CONCERNING CATTLE TRANSPORTATION.

Proclamation Quarantining Certain Localities on Account of Texas Fever.

STATE OF KANSAS, EXECUTIVE DEPARTMENT,
TOPEKA, February 25, 1899.

WHEREAS, As per "regulations concerning cattle transportation," by the United States department of agriculture, under date of December 19, and special orders of December 20, 1898, modifying quarantine line for the year 1899, that a contagious and infectious disease, known as splenic or Southern fever, exists among cattle in the United States in the area hereinafter set forth:

Now, THEREFORE, I, W. E. Stanley, governor of the state of Kansas, for the purpose of preventing the introduction and spread of said disease in this state, do, by virtue of the authority in me vested, hereby proclaim that any cattle imported into this state from all that country lying south or below a line—

Beginning at the northwest corner of the state of California; thence east, south and southeasterly along the boundary line of said state of California to the southeastern corner of said state...

And no cattle from the above-described infected area shall be allowed to come into the state of Kansas, except as provided by the rules and regulations of the Live-Stock Sanitary Commission of this state.

February 25, 1899.

W. E. STANLEY, *Governor of Kansas.*

BY THE GOVERNOR:
[SEAL.]   GEO. A. CLARK, *Secretary of State.*
BY HILL P. WILSON, *Assistant Secretary.*

Affidavit and Application for Admission of Cattle to Kansas.
REGULATIONS 1899.

State of _____, County of _____, ss.

Personally appeared before me, the County Clerk (or a Notary Public) in and for the County and State aforesaid,

_____, *of lawful age, who, being duly sworn, on his oath says, that he is a citizen of the County of* _____ *and State of* _____; *and that of his personal knowledge he knows* _____ *head of* _____ *cattle, marked* _____ *and branded* _____ *of the County of* _____, *State of* _____; *and that the above-described cattle have been held in the pasture owned—leased by* _____ *in the County of* _____, *State of* _____, *since the 1st day of January, 1899, and that said cattle are now healthy, and have not come in contact with or been exposed in any manner to any cattle that have come from east or south of the quarantine line since said quarantine line was established by the Live-Stock Sanitary Commission of Kansas, on the 1st day of January, 1899, and that no contagious or infectious disease to which cattle are subject is known to exist in said pasture or vicinity, and that said cattle are free from Texas-fever ticks (Boophilus bovis).*

_____
Owner—Manager.

Subscribed and sworn to before me, this _____ *day of* _____ *1899.*

_____
County Clerk—Notary Public.

I, this day, make application for a permit to ship—drive the above-described cattle to _____, *Kansas, via* _____ *Railroad.*

These cattle will be shipped in _____ *trains, consigned to* _____

_____
Owner—Manager.

In 1899, Texas fever was just as menacing as it had been during the Chisholm Trail times. On the left is a notice about quarantine regulations and on the right is a permission-request form to bring cattle into Kansas.

produced; as a result, Texas fever continued to kill cattle. The farmers and ranchers became so enraged that they often shot longhorns on sight, without asking for a certificate.

Once again, the cattle were caught in the middle. Rustlers wanted them. Native Americans wanted them. Buffalo wanted a piece of them, and Kansas wanted them dead. The cloud of dust on the horizon was, above all else, bad news for the longhorns.

Cowboys encountered yet one more hazard on the Chisholm Trail. For greenies, it was what they remembered most about trailing cattle—and why they gave up cowboy life after one drive. For longhorns, it was the worst experience possible.

A drawing of a stampede.

It was the worst thing that could happen on the Long Drive, and there was no way to prepare for it. It could happen at any time, and it could last for an hour or a day. It was terror, horror, pain, and death all rolled into one—accompanied by the sounds of bones breaking, longhorns screaming, horses dying, and men yelling. When three thousand longhorns were totally out of control and running like wild animals, it was called a "stampede," as in "STAM-PEEEEEEDE!!!"

Stampedes occurred on the entire length of the Chisholm Trail. Cattle rustlers threw stones into herds at night to start one so they could steal the strays. Native Americans waved red cloth in the air to start one so they could collect stragglers. The smell of buffalo made longhorns run. Gunfire in Kansas made longhorns run. They ran at rivers when they refused to cross. They ran during storms when lightning struck their horns. Like all wild animals, longhorns were highly sensitive to their environment, and they became even more nervous in unfamiliar territory. When something alarmed them, they ran to stay alive, as they had for thirty years in Texas.

A stampede wasn't like the chase in west Texas, which involved a hundred longhorns running in a line. A stampede on the Chisholm Trail meant three thousand longhorns running in five different directions: complete panic and chaos. The earth was ripped up and thrown in a cowboy's face. He rode as fast as the mustang could go to reach the lead steers, but on the way he found that longhorns were on both sides of him, ripping his mount to pieces. Death was only seconds away, and it was a horrible death because he could see it coming. As the rider and mustang were knocked down and trampled, longhorns tripped over the bodies and were trampled themselves. Beneath the roar of the herd, men and animals screamed in pain.

A stampede was stopped by turning the lead steers and getting the cattle to circle. It could be accomplished in fifteen minutes if there was only one run in one direction. But any obstacle along the way—a tree, a mound of dirt, a longhorn that had fallen—would cause the run to split and split again. When the groups came back together, they collided at right angles, gouging each other and crushing cowboys and their mounts. If there were buffalo in the area, they could be counted on to attack stampeding longhorns. The goring took place at full gallop, and greenies steered clear of the killing; their horses wouldn't approach anyway. It was an act of suicide to try to stop this form of madness.

A stampede was terrifying because it started in a split second. There was no time to think, organize, or ask the boss for advice. A cowboy was useless if he didn't get on a horse within a minute, and it was over for him if he was on foot and the herd was headed his way.

If a greenie was lucky, he experienced his first stampede during the day while trailing the herd; at least he could see the start of it and the direction of the cattle.

If it came at night after a few hours of sleep, it hit with the suddenness of a bomb. Startled out of sleep, he grabbed his saddle and ran with the other men to the remuda. His first priority was to get a horse and get mounted before all the horses scattered. Then he tried to understand the orders being screamed at him in the dark. He rode as fast as he could in the direction of the herd and hoped that others knew what they were doing—because he didn't, and he was scared. When the stillness of the night was broken by three thousand longhorns suddenly running at full speed, it sounded like thunder and death. For most cowboys this was the worst moment in their lives.

A herd might stampede thirty times during the Long Drive, and some ran more than a hundred times. Ben Ferguson's herd stampeded six times in the first eight days, which wasn't unusual for the first week, before the cattle were trail broken. But even after being broken, they continued to run when something frightened them, meaning they weren't broken at all and were still wild, running as a unit to escape danger. Consequently, after five or six stampedes, a certain apprehension set in. The cowboys changed. They assumed the characteristics of the animals they sought to control—jumpy, a little on edge.

Albert Branshaw, a greenie, left an account of his first stampede. He was on night patrol when he noticed that all the cattle were lying down with the exception of one large steer. "While I was looking at him," Branshaw said, "he leaped into the air, came down and hit the ground with a heavy thud, and gave a grunt where he sounded like a hog. That was the signal. The whole herd was up and running—and heading right for me. My horse gave a lunge, jerked loose from me, and was away. I barely had time to climb into an oak tree. The cattle went by like a hurricane, hitting the tree with their horns. It took us all night to stop the run." The stampede was typical because the cattle were off in a second and longhorns were killed. Eleven died in the run. Two mustangs died, and two cowboys suffered broken legs. A boss could easily lose three hundred longhorns in stampedes.

The cowboys cursed the cattle when they ran, as if the longhorns were supposed to know that they were safe while being trailed and didn't need to run. In fact, they had no other choice but to run, and they suffered the most. Eighty-two in Don Westly's herd died when they plunged into a river. One hundred and ten in C. C. Tate's herd died when they hit a ditch, tripped, and were crushed by others running over them. At the Brazos River in 1876, the Wilson brothers bedded down a herd that was jumpy from a series of storms. They ran, and in trying to turn the herd in darkness, riders mistakenly forced the animals over a cliff and into a deep ravine. One by one the longhorns were sent tumbling down—twenty-seven hundred died. The trail boss William O'Neal described the aftermath of many stampedes: "We rode over carcasses of cattle as flat as the ground where they were laying. They had fallen or got knocked down, and then thousands of hoofs had tromped over them."

Stampedes dominated trail accounts and the carnage broke a cowboy's heart. Whether a greenie or a seasoned hand, the cowboy had come to respect the longhorns for their toughness and desire to be free. To see them wasted, to see their mangled bodies in a pile, was more than a cowboy could take. Teddy White said, "I wondered whether it was worth it. The sight of these brave animals, dead and dying, made grown men cry, and I was among them." Had the longhorns known what awaited them on the Long Drive, they might have wished for a bullet in the head in San Antonio. Like the roan that Rocky Reagan described as dropping dead at the sight of a ranch, they might have refused to take one step toward Kansas.

So a herd moving up the Chisholm Trail shrank in numbers each week until it reached Kansas—if it ever made it that far. By the time the cattle got to the railroad or near it, farmers and ranchers left the animals alone, as they would soon be leaving the state.

In summertime temperatures of one hundred degrees,

the longhorns were driven into holding pens, sweating profusely and thinned from the drive. On average, they lost 25 percent of their weight during the trip, and frequently more, depending on the number of stampedes. After entering the pens, the weaker cattle plopped to the ground, while steers and mossy horns looked around with glazed eyes—still leaders but now with nowhere to lead. At this point in his life, the greenie was a cowboy. His hardened face and sullen eyes were proof that he had completed the Long Drive.

If the pens were full, and they frequently were, the cowboy spent another month holding the herd miles from the train station and waiting a turn for shipping. He soon discovered that this was an ideal setting for another stampede. The sound of the train set them off. Loud people in stagecoaches set them off. Hunger, thirst, and

A Hollywood version of a cow camp after a stampede.

the burning sun made them run. When a herd stampeded into another herd, and the two then ran into a third, there was no name for it—at least, not one that can be repeated. In one case, it took six outfits ten days to separate the cattle. More than three hundred died in the run, and thirty mustangs were trampled to death.

It was a difficult time for the mustangs left in the remuda. On average, they had worked two shifts of four hours every day since the spring. The small horses often carried large men who were strong enough to rope a longhorn and pull it to the ground. The mustangs had had no corn or other feed and had to rely on wild grasses to keep up strength. By the time they were in Kansas near the railroad, they might have two more stampedes left in them, but no more. Drained of energy and strength beyond recovery, their useful life had been used up in four months. At the end of the Long Drive, they might be butchered or released into the wild to compete with healthy mustangs, cougars, and wolves.

Artist's rendering of loading longhorns into a Kansas railroad car.

At last, the drive ended when longhorns were loaded into the railroad cars. Fighting to the end, they refused to enter the wooden chutes that extended from the ground up to the cars. The cowboys shoved the outlaws, pulled them by the horns, and jabbed them in the rear with railroad spikes. Some cattle slammed their horns against the sides of the chute, then reared up and kicked the sides down. Some jumped over the sides, broke their legs in the fall, and had to be shot. Mossy horns, steers, and other outlaws who still wouldn't obey had their horns chopped off or knocked off with heavy sticks. The pain broke their spirit, and the loss of their horns allowed for the shipment of more cattle in a car.

Now the greenie was done. He didn't have to smell longhorns anymore or worry about the next crisis. He was paid about $125, maybe the most money he ever had at one time, and he was eager to put the last four months behind him. Typically, he ended cowboy life in Abilene, Dodge City, Wichita, or one of the other cow towns that had been created to take his pay. It took about two weeks to complete the task. He spent his wages on whiskey, gambling, and carousing, and when his fun ended he had

A drawing of Abilene, Kansas, the first big "cow town."

67

just enough money for the return trip home. Riding away from cowboy life, he sang:

Good-bye, old trail boss, I wish you no harm;
I'm quittin' this business to go on a farm.
I'll sell my old saddle and buy me a plow;
And never, no never, will I rope another cow.

Dodge City, a typical trailhead town. The inset is the cover of a five-cent novel glamorizing the cowboy life.

In spite of its hazards, the Long Drive was a success in that most of the cattle that were trailed made it to market. About 85 percent of the longhorns reached Kansas, some five million over the course of twenty years, and the Long Drive ended when virtually all of the cattle in west Texas had been caught and trailed north. Nearly a million longhorns died on the trail and some 800,000

The Chicago stockyards.

mustangs died. Of the thirty-five thousand cowboys who trailed longhorns to Kansas, about one thousand died along the way; another two hundred died in the cow hunt. Stampedes killed more men and animals than all other hazards combined. The danger of the job and low pay were the reasons why most cowboys abandoned the work.

Investors in America and Europe financed the Long Drive; they paid men to capture longhorns and drive them to Kansas, hoping that enough would survive to make the enterprise profitable. It was. Even after losing cattle on the trail, the average profit for a herd of three thousand was $100,000. The total profit over twenty years was $180 million. Many herds were slaughtered in Chicago, which became a major city because of its meatpacking plants, and the new business led to the creation of refrigerated railroad cars and ships, which carried beef to Europe. The Long Drive shifted the American and European diet to beef, and longhorns led to the development of the range cattle industry.

Some longhorns driven north on the Chisholm Trail were sold to ranchers in Nebraska, Wyoming, Montana, and the Dakotas. Most of the buyers were just starting ranches, while others had small stocks of Angus cattle and wanted to expand their ranches. The ranchers kept some longhorns until they were fattened and then sold them, making a profit on the extra bulk of the animals. The remaining cattle were used to increase stock, and some offspring were kept for breeding. By the end of the Long Drive, the range cattle industry was well established, and prospects for the future looked good. The tough longhorns could survive the harsh winters in the northern plains. Or so it was believed.

The first real test came in 1885, in the first month of the last year of the Long Drive. At that time, the northern plains were still unfenced and longhorns were free to move at will. When it was cold and the grass was frozen, they would move, or "drift," and most drifts were to the south, as storms pushed the cattle southward to warmer temperatures. In January of 1885, a four-day storm of ice and snow started a drift in all areas from the Dakotas to the Indian Territory. Storm after storm followed, in one of the coldest winters in recorded history. From a distance of more than a thousand miles, the cattle came sweeping down, as if wanting to return home to Texas.

Hundreds of thousands swept across Kansas until they

A portrait of the 1885 "Big Die-Up," in which countless cattle died of exposure.

encountered a "drift fence" just above the southern border of the state. It was six feet high and made of logs, boards, and barbed wire. It stretched for 170 miles, and its purpose was to keep the unwanted longhorns away from railroads and other stock. When they encountered the fence, the animals were freezing: to survive, the leaders tried to knock the barrier down. Using all their muscle, they rammed and rammed the fence until they lost their strength and fell down. Others stumbled over the dead and were trampled themselves, until the pile was so high that it acted as an overpass—the remaining cattle climbed over the dead bodies and scaled the fence. Piles of dead cattle marked every mile of the fence, and still the wind and snow were unrelenting. The scene was repeated at a second drift fence farther south in the Indian Territory.

Ranchers called the drift of '85 the "Big Die-Up." Seventy-five percent of the range cattle died, most of them frozen to death. The losses numbered in the millions and put many ranchers out of business.

In March, the last of the longhorns in Texas were trailed to Kansas. By then, the carcasses along the Chisholm Trail from the Die-Up were starting to thaw, and the longhorns ran to escape from what they could see and smell. For cowboys and longhorns, the last Long Drive ended with more than the usual sadness: the Chisholm Trail looked like one long graveyard. There was another drift in the winter of 1886, when more than a million cattle died. Afterward, barbed wire fences kept the longhorns confined, and they were sheltered during the winter months.

The longhorns that survived on the northern ranges were eventually bred out of existence. Compared to the beef of Angus breeds, longhorn meat was tough and stringy. They were crossed with Herefords to produce the round-bellied, white-faced cattle of today. They have the

Today's farm-raised longhorns.

Charley Siringo, a professional cowboy.

weight of the longhorn but the tender meat of Angus cattle. By the 1890s, longhorns were nearly extinct. At their low point, they numbered less than five hundred but were bred back into existence in the twentieth century. (Mustangs and buffalo were also nearly extinct and were bred back in the twentieth century.)

Those cowboys who had worked with wild longhorns for years were sad to see the passing of the animal and the end of the cowboy way of life, meaning the cow hunt and the Long Drive. The cowboy Frank Collinson said, "Some folks pity the bull in the ring in Mexican bullfights. I pity the Texas longhorns that came to such a terrible end, after weathering the trail so nobly, and we with them. I'm sorry that they are gone." In 1882, Charley Siringo complained, "Cattle are becoming so tame, from being bred up with short horns, that it requires very little skill and knowledge to be a cowboy. I believe the day is not far distant when cowboys will be armed with prod-poles to punch cattle out of their way. The Winchester Gun Company will then have to go out of business or open up a prod-pole factory."

Two photographs of authentic cowboys from the waning days of the Wild West.

Who, then, was this character called the cowboy? At the start, he was Mexican and African American, and later he was an Anglo. Typically, he was a greenie who was overworked, underpaid, often bored, and sometimes terrified. He was sleepy. He was sore. He didn't like nonwhites, swore on nearly every occasion, and blew his pay on alcohol and other diversions. If he didn't die in the work, he quit after one drive. He didn't like being a cowboy.

The other cowboy—the brush popper, trail boss, pointer, and swing man—stayed with the work year after year because it was all he knew how to do and he lacked the skill or education for other kinds of work. These men were resigned to a lowly existence of working for little more than food and clothing. "I put in eighteen years on the trail," said an old cowboy, "and all I have to show for it is a pair of high-heeled boots and $4.80 worth of clothes, so there you are."

Above all else, the cowboy was no hero in his time, and he never asked to be made into one in the future. He was what he was—for his time—a man on a horse who conquered a wild animal and sang,

> *I woke up one morning on the Old Chisholm Trail,*
> *Rope in my hand and a cow by the tail.*
> *Feet in the stirrups and seat in the saddle,*
> *I hung and rattled with them Longhorn cattle.*

Bibliographic Note

The image of the American cowboy is discussed in William W. Savage, Jr., *The Cowboy Hero: His Image in American History and Culture* (Norman, OK: University of Oklahoma Press, 1979). Other useful sources include Mody C. Boatright, "The Cowboy Enters the Movies," in Wilson M. Hudson and Allen Maxwell, eds., *The Sunny Slopes of Long Ago* (Dallas: Southern Methodist University Press, 1966); Douglas Branch, *The Cowboy and His Interpreters* (New York: Cooper Square Publishers, 1961); Ralph Brauer and Donna Brauer, *The Horse, the Gun, and the Piece of Property: Changing Images of the TV Western* (Bowling Green, OH: Bowling Green State University Popular Press, 1975); Jenni Calder, *There Must Be a Lone Ranger: The American West in Film and in Reality* (New York: Taplinger Publishing Company, 1975); Joe B. Frantz and Julian Ernest Choate, Jr., *The American Cowboy: The Myth and the Reality* (Norman, OK: University of Oklahoma Press, 1955); Robert Heide and John Gilman, *Cowboy Collectibles* (New York: Harper and Row, 1962); Don Russell, "The Cowboy: From Black Hat to White," *Red River Valley Historical Review* 2 (spring 1975); Kent Ladd Steckmesser, *The Western Hero in History and Legend* (Norman, OK: University of Oklahoma Press, 1997); and Jack Weston, "The Cowboy Myth," in *The Real American Cowboy* (New York: New Amsterdam Books, 1990).

For information on the first cowboys, see Philip Durham and Everett L. Jones, *The Negro Cowboys* (Lincoln, NE: University of Nebraska Press, 1983); Arnold R. Rojas, *These Were the Vaqueros* (Shafter, CA: Charles Hitchcock, 1974); John D. Young and J. Frank Dobie, *A Vaquero of the Brush Country: The Life and Times of John D. Young* (Dallas: University of Texas Press, 1999); and Charles Zurhorst, *The First Cowboys and Those Who Followed* (New York: Abelard-Schuman Ltd., 1973).

For the origin of the longhorn, the cow hunt, and the

Long Drive, information was drawn from the following sources: Ralph Compton, *The Chisholm Trail* (New York: St. Martin's Press, 1993); Don Cusic, *Cowboys and the Wild West: An A–Z Guide from the Chisholm Trail to the Silver Screen* (New York: Facts on File, 1994); J. Frank Dobie, *Cow People* (Boston: Little, Brown and Co., 1964); J. Frank Dobie, *The Longhorns* (Dallas: University of Texas Press, 1980); Harry Sinclair Drago, *Great American Cattle Trails* (New York: Bramhall House, 1965); Wayne Gard, *The Chisholm Trail* (Norman, OK: University of Oklahoma Press, 1954); Ernest Staples Osgood, *The Day of the Cattleman* (Chicago: University of Chicago Press, 1957); and Don Worcester, *The Chisholm Trail: High Road of the Cattle Kingdom* (Lincoln, NE: University of Nebraska Press, 1980).

For firsthand accounts of cowboy life, see Ramon F. Adams, *The Rampaging Herd: A Bibliography of Books and Pamphlets on Men and Events in the Cattle Industry* (Norman, OK: University of Oklahoma Press, 1959). Firsthand information was drawn from the following sources: E. C. Abbott and Helena Huntington Smith, *We Pointed Them North: Recollections of a Cowpuncher* (Norman, OK: University of Oklahoma Press, 1955); Andy Adams, *The Log of a Cowboy* (Boston: Houghton Mifflin Company, 1903); Ramon F. Adams, *The Old-Time Cowhand* (New York: Macmillan, 1961); Frank Collinson, *Life in the Saddle,* ed. Mary Whatley Clarke (Norman, OK: University of Oklahoma Press, 1968); James Henry Cook, *Longhorn Cowboy,* ed. Howard R. Driggs (New York: G. P. Putnam's Sons, 1942); Chris Emmett, *Shanghai Pierce: A Fair Likeness* (Norman, OK: University of Oklahoma Press, 1953); Baylis John Fletcher, *Up the Trail in '79* (Norman, OK: University of Oklahoma Press, 1968); Charles Goodnight, "Managing a Trail Herd in the Early Days," *Frontier Times* (November 1929); Wilson M. Hudson, *Andy Adams: His Life and Writings* (Dallas: Southern Methodist University Press, 1964); John Marvin Hunter, ed., *Trail Drivers of Texas* (Nashville: Cokesbury Press, 1925); Bob Kennon, as told to Ramon F. Adams, *From the Pecos to the Powder: A Cowboy's Autobiography* (Norman, OK: University of Oklahoma Press, 1965); J. L. McCaleb, "A Texas Boy's First Experience on the Trail," *Frontier Times*

(October 1927); Joseph G. McCoy, *Historic Sketches of the Cattle Trade of the West and Southwest,* ed. Ralph P. Bieber (Lincoln, NE: University of Nebraska Press, 1985); Charles Clement Post, *Ten Years a Cowboy* (Chicago: Rhodes and McClure Publishing Company, 1888); E. B. Ritchie, "A Trail Driver Who Kept a Diary," *Cattleman* (August 1932); William W. Savage, Jr., ed., *Cowboy Life: Reconstructing an American Myth* (Norman, OK: University of Oklahoma Press, 1975); Charles A. Siringo, *A Texas Cow Boy; or, Fifteen Years on the Hurricane Deck of a Spanish Pony* (Chicago: Rand, McNally and Co., 1886); Charles A. Siringo, *A Lone Star Cowboy* (published by author, 1919); and Nellie Snyder Yost, ed., *Boss Cowman: The Recollections of Ed Lemmon, 1857–1946* (Lincoln, NE: University of Nebraska Press, 1969).

Cow-town life is described in Robert R. Dykstra, "Ellsworth, 1869–1875: The Rise and Fall of a Kansas Cow Town," *Kansas Historical Quarterly* (summer 1961); Robert R. Dykstra, "The Last Days of 'Texan' Abilene," *Agricultural History* (July 1960); Odie B. Faulk, *Dodge City: The Most Western Town of All* (New York: Oxford University Press, 1977); Nyle H. Miller and Joseph W. Snell, *Great Gunfighters of the Kansas Cowtowns* (Lincoln, NE: University of Nebraska Press, 1967); F. B. Streeter, *Prairie Trails and Cow Towns* (Boston: Chapman and Grimes, 1936); and Stanley Vestal, *Queen of Cowtowns: Dodge City, "The Wickedest Little City in America," 1872–1886* (New York: Harper, 1952). For the Big Die-Up of 1885, see Dobie, *The Longhorns,* and Worcester, *The Chisholm Trail.* Part of the importance of the Long Drive is detailed in Wayne Gard, "The Impact of the Cattle Trails," *Southwestern Historical Quarterly* (July 1967).

For cowboy songs, stories, and general reference, see Katie Lee, *Ten Thousand Goddam Cattle: A History of the American Cowboy in Song, Story and Verse* (Flagstaff, AZ: Northland Press, 1976) and Richard W. Slatta, *The Cowboy Encyclopedia* (Santa Barbara, CA: ABC-CLIO, 1994).

Acknowledgments

I wish to thank the librarians who helped locate research materials at the Huntington Library in San Marino, the University of California at Los Angeles, and California State University, Bakersfield. Camille Gavin critiqued the manuscript prior to publication. Some quotations were edited for clarity.

*Page numbers in **boldface** refer to illustrations.*

T

V

W

Jerry Stanley is the author of several highly praised books for young readers, including *Children of the Dust Bowl,* winner of the Orbis Pictus Award; *Digger: The Tragic Fate of the California Indians from the Missions to the Gold Rush,* an Orbis Pictus Award Honor Book; *I Am an American,* an ALA Notable Book; and *Hurry Freedom: African Americans in Gold Rush California,* a National Book Award nominee and winner of the Orbis Pictus Award. A former professor of history at California State University, he lives in Bakersfield, California.